It's a Mathematical

Maths
in Nature

Thanks to the creative team:

Senior Editor: Alice Peebles
Illustration: Dan Newman
Fact checking: Tom Jackson
Picture Research: Nic Dean
Design: Perfect Bound Ltd

First published in Great Britain in 2018
by Hungry Tomato Ltd
PO Box 181
Edenbridge
Kent, TN8 9DP

A CIP catalogue record for this book is
available from the British Library.

ISBN 978-1-912108-54-1

Printed and bound in China

Discover more at
www.hungrytomato.com

It's a Mathematical World

Maths in Nature

by Nancy Dickmann

HUNGRY
TOMATO™

Contents

Maths
All Around Us

Maths is a subject you study at school, but it's so much more than that. Maths can be found everywhere in the world around us.

Patterns in nature

Did you know that there are shapes in a beehive and number **patterns** in a sunflower? Or that the shape of a hurricane is similar to the shape of a **nautilus** shell? Nature is constantly changing and evolving as plants and animals find new ways to survive. But no matter how much they change, they still follow many of the basic rules of maths.

A hurricane's shape may look random, but it usually follows a mathematical pattern.

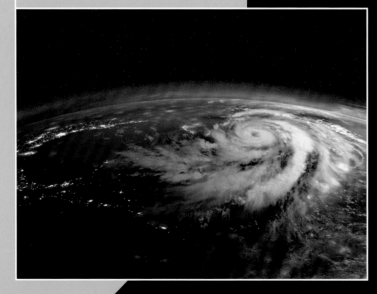

A fly's eyes are made up of tiny, identical parts. They are arranged in orderly patterns.

Mirror Image

Animals come in all shapes and sizes, but many of them have one thing in common: their bodies are symmetrical.

Super symmetry

If an object is symmetrical, it means that some of its parts are shaped exactly like others. The simplest type of symmetry is called 'reflection symmetry' or **bilateral symmetry**. In an object with this type of symmetry, you can draw a line down the middle of it. The halves on each side will be mirror images of each other. With a dog, you could draw a line down its back, from its nose to the tip of its tail. Each half would be a perfect reflection of the other.

A stag beetle has bilateral symmetry – each side has three legs, one antenna, one pincer and one wing.

A zebra's head is symmetrical, with one ear, one eye and one nostril on each side.

Symmetry in nature

No one is exactly sure why so many animals have bilateral symmetry. One possible reason is that having both sides of the body the same makes it easier to move forwards. Think about building a model car with wheels of different sizes – it will have a hard time driving in a straight line.

Even animals that are symmetrical on the outside aren't always symmetrical on the inside. A few of your body's **organs**, such as the kidneys, come in pairs, but your stomach and intestines aren't symmetrical at all.

Humans have bilateral symmetry on the outside, but inside it's a different story.

Maths in action!

Have a go at using symmetry to finish a picture. Trace this drawing of a penguin onto a sheet of paper, then try to fill in the other side. It should be a mirror image of the first side. Adding grid lines will make it easier to make the two halves match up.

In the Round

*There are different types of symmetry. In addition to bilateral symmetry, many animals and plants, such as sea urchins and oranges, show a type called **radial symmetry**, shown here.*

Turn, turn, turn

Radial symmetry is also called rotational symmetry. If you take an object with radial symmetry and **rotate** it by a certain amount, it will look exactly the same. An object with bilateral symmetry has just one line of symmetry, but an object with radial symmetry can have three, four, five or even more lines. The number shows how many times it can be rotated in a circle and still look the same.

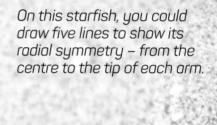

On this starfish, you could draw five lines to show its radial symmetry – from the centre to the tip of each arm.

The body of an orb weaver spider has bilateral symmetry, but it spins a web with radial symmetry.

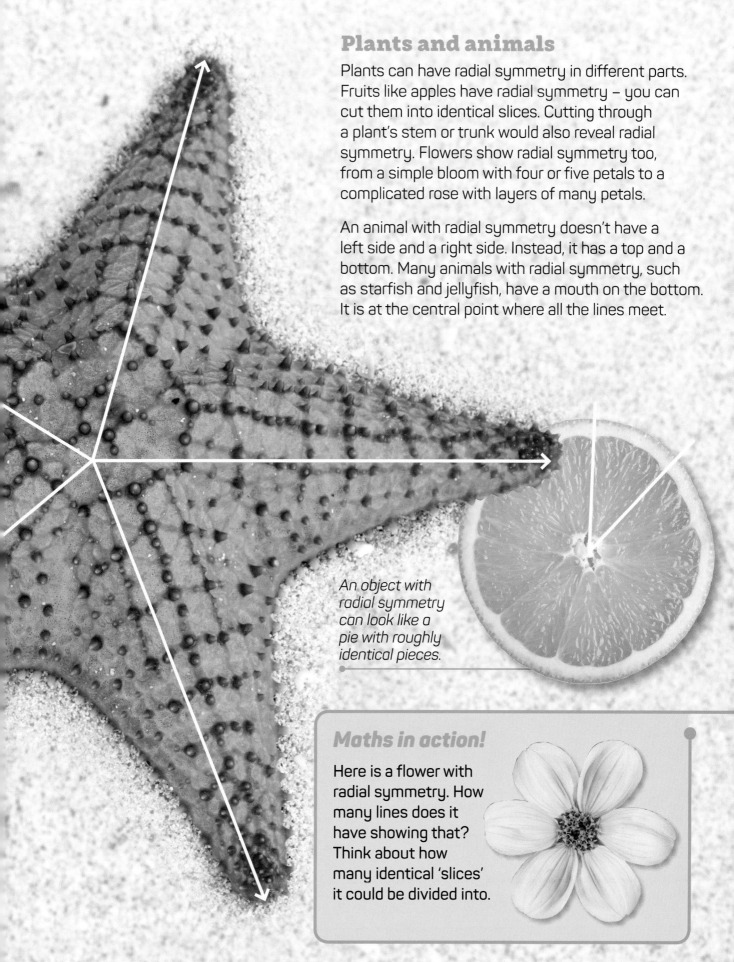

Plants and animals

Plants can have radial symmetry in different parts. Fruits like apples have radial symmetry – you can cut them into identical slices. Cutting through a plant's stem or trunk would also reveal radial symmetry. Flowers show radial symmetry too, from a simple bloom with four or five petals to a complicated rose with layers of many petals.

An animal with radial symmetry doesn't have a left side and a right side. Instead, it has a top and a bottom. Many animals with radial symmetry, such as starfish and jellyfish, have a mouth on the bottom. It is at the central point where all the lines meet.

An object with radial symmetry can look like a pie with roughly identical pieces.

Maths in action!

Here is a flower with radial symmetry. How many lines does it have showing that? Think about how many identical 'slices' it could be divided into.

Adding Up

*Some strings of numbers can form patterns. There is one **sequence** of numbers that pops up throughout the natural world.*

An Italian idea

An Italian **mathematician** known as Fibonacci first wrote about the sequence in 1202. Starting with 0 and 1, he continued the sequence of numbers. Each number was the sum of the two numbers that came before, so after 0 and 1 came 1. He added 1 and 1 to get 2, then added 1 and 2 to get 3. The sequence goes: 0, 1, 1, 2, 3, 5, 8, 13, and continues from there:

$$0 + 1 = 1$$
$$1 + 1 = 2$$
$$1 + 2 = 3$$
$$2 + 3 = 5$$
$$3 + 5 = 8$$
$$5 + 8 = 13 \ldots$$

The parts of a pine cone are also arranged in spirals. The number of spirals is usually a Fibonacci number.

Numbers in nature

Numbers in the Fibonacci sequence often appear in nature. On many flowers, the number of petals is a **Fibonacci number**. Other flowers have Fibonacci numbers in the seeds at the centre. In a sunflower, the seeds **spiral** out from the centre. The number of spirals is nearly always a Fibonacci number.

Having seeds arranged in spirals is a way of keeping the seeds evenly packed throughout the seed head. You can follow the spirals from left to right, or from right to left. Either way, you will get a Fibonacci number. Often, the two totals will be next to each other in the Fibonacci sequence.

A single sunflower can have more than 1,000 seeds set in spirals. You can follow the spirals by starting at the centre and moving out to the edge.

Maths in action!

Here are some numbers in the Fibonacci sequence. Can you work out the next four?

13, 21, 34, ___, ___, ___, ___

Remember that each number is the sum of the two previous numbers.

The Golden Ratio

A **ratio** is the relationship between two numbers. There is one particular ratio that is so special it is called the 'golden ratio'.

Finding a ratio

When two numbers are in the golden ratio, you can take the larger number and divide it by the smaller number. Then, if you add the two numbers together and divide by the larger number, you'll get the same result. Both division problems will equal approximately 1.618, which is the golden ratio. Mathematicians use the Greek letter phi (written φ) to represent it.

If you take any two **adjacent** numbers from the Fibonacci sequence, you'll find that their relationship is very close to the golden ratio. The further you get along the sequence, the closer the ratio is to phi.

So, taking two numbers from the previous page (use a calculator):
a) 13 ÷ 8 = 1.625
b) 13 + 8 = 21. Then divide this sum by the larger number: 21 ÷ 13 = 1.615

Both of the answers are very close to the golden ratio.

The nautilus grows by adding new chambers in its shell, creating a shape that is close to a golden spiral.

*The orange shape is a **golden rectangle**. Adding the purple square makes a larger golden rectangle.*

The golden spiral

Rectangles have two equal long sides and two equal short sides. A golden rectangle has side lengths that are in the golden ratio. Adding a square that matches the longer side makes a larger golden rectangle. When golden rectangles of increasing size join together, they form a golden spiral. There are many examples of this in nature, such as the shell of the nautilus (left).

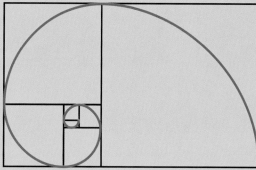

A golden spiral connects a series of golden rectangles of increasing size.

Hurricane clouds and even galaxies can form shapes resembling a golden spiral.

Maths in action!

Measure the distance from the ground to your belly button, and then the distance from your belly button to the top of your head. Use a calculator to work out the ratios: divide the first number by the second. How close is it to 1.618?

Geometric Homes

A beehive is a neat, orderly place. If you look closely, you'll see that the honeycomb is made of rows of six-sided shapes.

Super shapes

A shape that is flat is called a two-dimensional (2D) shape. It has two dimensions – width and height – but no thickness. A 2D shape with six straight sides is called a **hexagon**. This is what honeycombs are made of. Honeycombs form a pattern called a **tessellation**. In a tessellation, shapes are repeated over and over, with no gaps between them.

In the hive

Each hexagon in a beehive is called a cell. The bees use them to store food, such as nectar and pollen. The young bees also grow and develop in the cells. But why are they hexagons?

A bee colony can produce dozens of kilograms of honey, so the honeycomb must be strong enough to hold it. The wax that forms the cells is made by the bees themselves. However, they need to eat a lot of honey to produce the wax. They can't waste honey – it's an important food source. A hexagon is the shape that uses the least amount of wax to hold the most weight.

There are many forms of tessellation in the natural world, on plants and animals. Although a snake's scales are not all the same size and shape, they fit together perfectly.

Maths in action!

Can you design your own tessellation? Choose a simple shape, such as a triangle, square or diamond. Draw it on card, then cut it out. You can trace around the edges over and over to create a tessellation. You will probably need to use more than one type of shape. This is fine, as long as the arrangement follows a regular pattern.

Rock Patterns

Tessellations are not just found in living things. Rock formations can have shapes arranged in patterns, too.

Giant's Causeway

On the coast of Northern Ireland lies Giant's Causeway, an area of 40,000 columns made of rock. Most of the columns are hexagon-shaped, and some are 12 metres tall. They fit tightly together in a pattern similar to the cells in a beehive.

The columns are made of basalt, a type of rock that forms when **lava** cools and hardens. As lava cools, it contracts (gets smaller). When this happens, it causes cracks that create the shape of the columns. Once one hexagonal column forms, many more tend to form around it.

Each 'step' in Giant's Causeway can be up to 50 centimetres across. One legend says it is a road built by a giant.

Tessellated pavements

A tessellated pavement is another form of rock that is cracked to form a pattern of shapes. They can look as neat and orderly as a carefully laid patio. Instead of lava, tessellated pavements are made from **sedimentary rock**. Tiny pieces of silt settle in a flat area, and over millions of years, they become squashed and turn into rock.

Tessellated pavements form when these rocks crack in different directions, forming patterns of squares, rectangles and other shapes. Wind and water **erode** the rock, making the patterns even more obvious.

This stunning landscape in Tasmania, Australia, is a perfect example of a tessellated pavement.

Maths in action!

If there are 40,000 columns in a formation like Giant's Causeway, and 70% of them are hexagon-shaped, how many columns are hexagons? You can use a calculator if you need to.

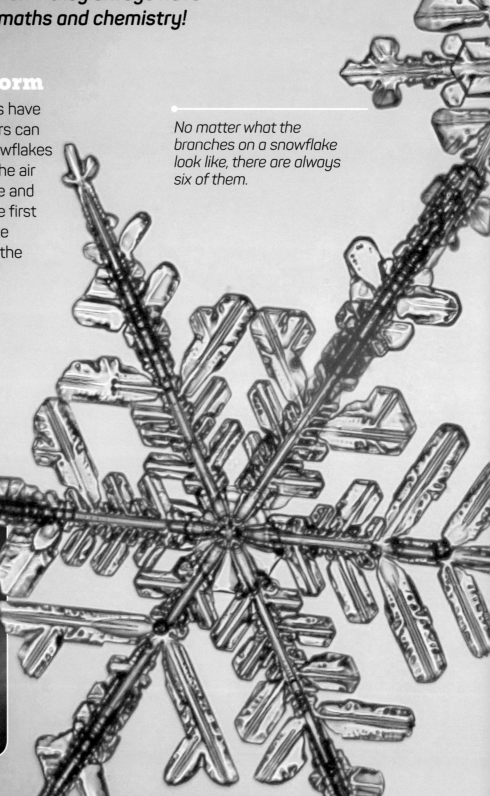

Let It Snow!

Every snowflake's shape is unique, but they do have one thing in common – they always have six sides. It's all about maths and chemistry!

How snowflakes form

The most familiar snowflakes have six branching arms, but others can be simple flat hexagons. Snowflakes form when **water vapour** in the air freezes directly into ice. More and more ice crystals form on the first crystal, making the snowflake bigger. As it grows, it follows the six-sided pattern begun by the very first crystal.

No matter what the branches on a snowflake look like, there are always six of them.

A fly's big eyes are made up of many smaller eyes. They are hexagon-shaped and arranged in patterns.

All about angles

An **angle** is a measure of a turn that is measured in degrees, shown by the symbol °. There are 360° in a full circle. Snowflakes are made of frozen water. Each **molecule** of water is made up of one oxygen **atom** and two hydrogen atoms. All water molecules are identical because the hydrogen atoms always attach to the oxygen atom in the same way. They always form an angle of 104°.

Water molecule

When water molecules join together, they arrange themselves in a certain way. Positive areas of the hydrogen atoms are attracted to the negative charge of an oxygen atom in a different molecule. They end up forming a ring of six molecules, making a hexagon shape.

Ring of water molecules

Maths in action!

A hexagon has six sides and six angles. The angles are all identical. The sum of all the angles is 720°. What is the measurement of each angle?

Fabulous Fractals

*Patterns are everywhere in nature, but some of the most amazing ones are **fractals**. These shapes repeat themselves at different scales, forming complex patterns.*

Branching out

A fractal takes a simple shape and then repeats it over and over. For example, a tree begins by a single sprout splitting into two or more branches. Each branch then branches again, and the newest branches split too. In a fully grown tree, tiny twigs and giant limbs form the same branching pattern. River systems, brain cells and the airways inside our lungs also form branching patterns.

A Romanesco broccoli forms a spiral that is linked to the Fibonacci sequence.

Big and small

Every tiny section of a fractal has the same shape as the whole object. Romanesco broccoli is a good example of this. Each spike of the broccoli is made up of smaller but identical spikes arranged in spiral patterns. And each of *these* smaller buds is made up of even smaller buds. It goes on and on, the same shape repeating itself over and over, getting smaller each time.

When frost forms on glass, it often naturally forms fractal patterns.

Each smaller 'leaf' on the frond of a fern is roughly the same shape as the frond itself.

Maths in action!

You can make your own fractal pattern! Draw a large triangle with sides of equal length. Make a dot halfway along each side and connect them to form a new triangle inside the original triangle. Colour it in, so that you are left with three white triangles surrounding it. Repeat the process in each of the white triangles to draw smaller triangles inside them. Keep going until your fractal pattern is too small to draw any more.

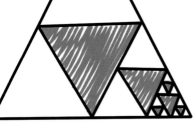

Beating the Cold

Some animals survive in hot places, and others thrive in cold. The secret is all down to body shape.

Volume vs. surface area

Any three-dimensional (3D) shape has **volume** and **surface area**. Volume is a measure of how much space it contains. Surface area is the total area of the shape's outer surface. For warm-blooded animals, the ratio between these two measurements is crucial.

Losing less heat helps a walrus stay warm in its icy home.

Cheetahs are long and thin. They have a lot of surface area in relation to their volume.

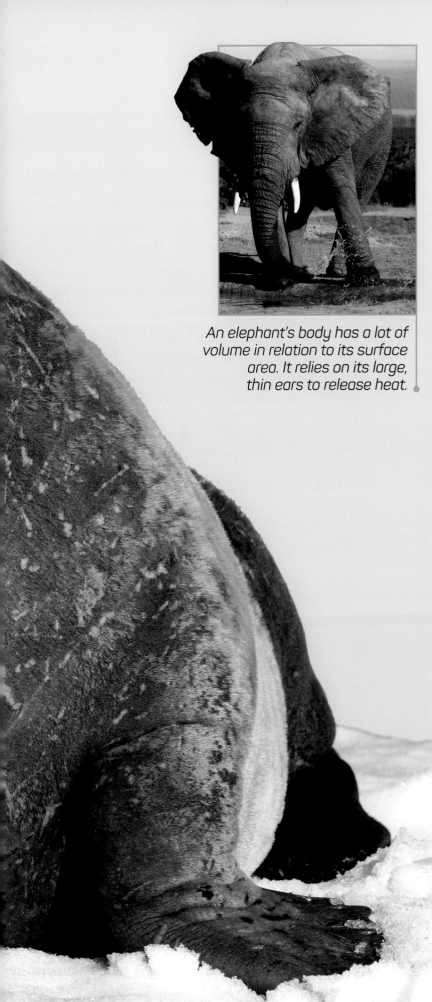

Hot and cold

Warm-blooded animals release heat through their skin. In a hot climate, this stops them overheating. But in a cold climate, releasing heat is a bad thing. The more heat that animals lose, the more food they need to eat to keep their bodies warm.

Small animals, such as mice, have a large surface area compared to their volume. But as an animal grows bigger and fatter, its volume increases faster than its surface area. A large animal like a walrus will have a smaller surface area in relation to its volume. So the mouse loses heat quickly and has to eat a lot to replace it. The walrus loses heat more slowly.

An elephant's body has a lot of volume in relation to its surface area. It relies on its large, thin ears to release heat.

Maths in action!

Imagine a cube with sides of 1 cm. Work out its surface area by adding up the area of each side. Then work out its volume by multiplying length x width x height. Now do the same for a cube with sides of 2 cm. What is the ratio between the surface area and the volume of the first cube? What is the ratio for the second cube?

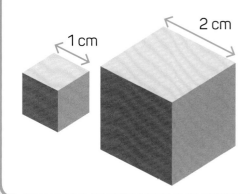

How Many Babies?

For most animals, producing young is a numbers game. Should they go high, or should they go low? It depends...

More or fewer?

There are species of fish and insects that produce millions of eggs in a single season. On the other hand, elephants take nearly two years to produce a single calf. But why do some animals produce so many young, and others so few?

The mola (also called the ocean sunfish) can produce 300 million eggs in a single season.

*A baby wildebeest must outrun **predators**, so it's able to walk within an hour of birth.*

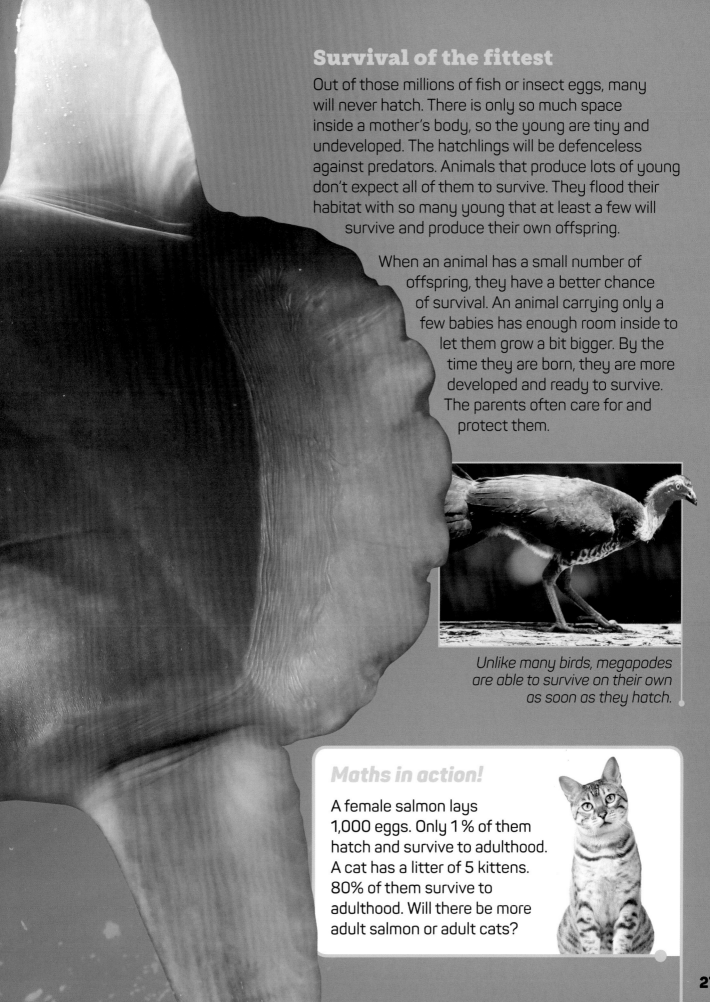

Survival of the fittest

Out of those millions of fish or insect eggs, many will never hatch. There is only so much space inside a mother's body, so the young are tiny and undeveloped. The hatchlings will be defenceless against predators. Animals that produce lots of young don't expect all of them to survive. They flood their habitat with so many young that at least a few will survive and produce their own offspring.

When an animal has a small number of offspring, they have a better chance of survival. An animal carrying only a few babies has enough room inside to let them grow a bit bigger. By the time they are born, they are more developed and ready to survive. The parents often care for and protect them.

Unlike many birds, megapodes are able to survive on their own as soon as they hatch.

Maths in action!

A female salmon lays 1,000 eggs. Only 1% of them hatch and survive to adulthood. A cat has a litter of 5 kittens. 80% of them survive to adulthood. Will there be more adult salmon or adult cats?

Maths in Action:
Answers & Tips

How did you get on with the 10 maths challenges? Here are the correct answers and some tips on how to work them out.

Page 9: Did you end up with a symmetrical drawing? Lay your finished drawing onto this one and see how they match up. Using grid lines breaks the picture up into smaller chunks and makes it easier to copy each chunk accurately.

Page 11: The flower has six lines. You could draw a line from the centre to the tip of each of the six petals, and end up with six equal 'slices'. So it could be rotated six times and still look the same.

Page 13: The next four numbers are 55, 89, 144, 233. Here's how you work it out:

$21 + 34 = 55$
$34 + 55 = 89$
$55 + 89 = 144$
$89 + 144 = 233$

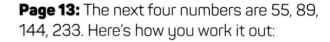

Page 15: There is no right answer to this question, as it all depends on your own height! An average 9-year-old might measure 87 cm from the ground to her belly button, and 55 cm from her belly button to the top of her head. Dividing the first number by the second gives 1.581, which is fairly close to the golden ratio of 1.618. How close was your own number?

Page 17: To check whether your drawing is a true tessellation, see if you can answer 'yes' to all these questions:

- Is your drawing completely covered with flat shapes, with no overlaps or gaps?
- Have you used the same shape or shapes over and over?
- At every vertex (a 'corner point' where shapes meet), is the pattern identical?

Page 19: There are 28,000 columns shaped like hexagons. To work this out, you need to find 70% of 40,000. 70% is equal to $\frac{70}{100}$, $\frac{7}{10}$ or 0.7, and plugging 40,000 x 0.7 into a calculator gives you 28,000.

If you want to work it out without a calculator, use place value to help by following these steps:

Start by finding 10% of 40,000. That means dividing it by 10, which is easily done by removing one of the zeroes to get 4,000.

You now need to multiply this number by 7 to find out what 70% would be.

If you know that 4 x 7 = 28, then it's easy to work out that 4,000 x 7 = 28,000.

Page 21: You know that a hexagon has six angles, and the sum of all the angles is 720° (degrees). The angles are all identical, so this is a simple division problem: 720 ÷ 6 = 120. (If you know that 12 x 6 = 72, then place value can help here, too!)

Page 23: Your triangle should look a bit like this. Depending on how big your paper is, you might have even more small triangles inside!

Page 25: Finding the ratios between the two cubes takes a few steps:

First, you need to find the surface area of the first cube. To find the area of each face, multiply length x width. In this case, that's 1 x 1 = 1. There are six identical faces, so 6 x 1 = 6. This means the cube has a surface area of 6 cm².

Next you need to find the cube's volume. This is done by multiplying length x width x height, so for this cube that's 1 x 1 x 1 = 1.

The cube has a volume of 1 cm³.

Now find the surface area of the second cube. To find the area of each face, multiply length x width. In this case, that's 2 x 2 = 4. There are six identical faces, so 6 x 4 = 24 cm².

The last measurement is the volume of the second cube. In this case, length x width x height is 2 x 2 x 2 = 8. The volume of the cube is 8 cm³.

Now for the ratio between the surface area and volume of each of the two cubes. For the first cube, the surface area is 6 and the volume is 1, giving a ratio of 6:1. For the second cube, the surface area is 24 and the volume is 8, giving a ratio of 24:8. To make it easier to compare the ratios, divide each number in the second ratio by 8 so that 24:8 becomes 3:1. This shows that as a cube gets bigger, the volume increases faster than the surface area.

Page 27: There will be more adult salmon. To work it out, first you need to find 1% of 1,000. 1% is equal to $\frac{1}{100}$ or 0.01, so 1% of 1,000 is 10. This is how many salmon will survive to adulthood.

Now for the kittens! You need to work out 80% of 5. 80% is equal to $\frac{8}{10}$ or 0.8, so 80% of 5 is 4. This is how many kittens will survive to adulthood.

Glossary

adjacent next to each other or side-by-side

angle the space between two lines that come from a central point. Angles are measured in degrees, written as °

atom the smallest unit of a substance that cannot be broken down into different substances

bilateral symmetry a type of symmetry in which each half of an object is a perfect mirror image of the other half

erode to wear away over time through the action of wind, water or temperature

Fibonacci number any number that is part of a sequence developed by the Italian mathematician known as Fibonacci

fractal a pattern in which the same shape is repeated at different scales to form a larger shape that is identical

golden rectangle a rectangle with sides that have lengths that are in the golden ratio

hexagon a two-dimensional shape with six flat sides

lava molten rock that comes from beneath Earth's crust

mathematician a person who works in mathematics

molecule the smallest possible unit of a substance that has all the properties of that substance

nautilus a type of mollusc with a spiral shell divided into chambers

organ part of a plant or animal that performs a particular task. The heart, lungs and stomach are all organs

pattern an arrangement of shapes, lines or numbers that can be repeated over and over

predator an animal that hunts other animals for food

radial symmetry a type of symmetry in which an object can be rotated by a certain amount and still look the same

ratio the relationship between two numbers. A ratio of 3 to 1 is written out as 3:1

rectangle a two-dimensional shape with four flat sides. The two long sides are of equal length, and the two short sides are of equal length

rotate to spin around a central axis

sedimentary rock a type of rock formed when soil, sand or other substances are laid down over time, then squashed to form solid rock

sequence a pattern in which one thing follows another

spiral a curve that circles around a central point, getting bigger as it gets farther from the centre

surface area the total area of the outside of a three-dimensional shape. To find an object's surface area, you add up the areas of each of its faces (sides)

tessellation an arrangement of two-dimensional shapes in a repeating pattern, with no gaps or overlaps

volume the total amount of space inside a three-dimensional shape

water vapour water in the form of gas

Amazing Maths Facts

Features on a human face – such as the eyes, nose and mouth – are often positioned according to the golden ratio.

The kiwi, a small bird from New Zealand, lays the largest egg in relation to its body size of all birds. When the egg hatches, the chick is fully feathered and independent.

The support threads in the web of an orb weaver spider are usually an equal distance from each other, resulting in an almost perfectly circular web.

Most species of starfish have five arms, but some types can have more than 40, like this Crown of Thorns Starfish. No matter how many arms a starfish has, they are arranged in a pattern that gives it radial symmetry.

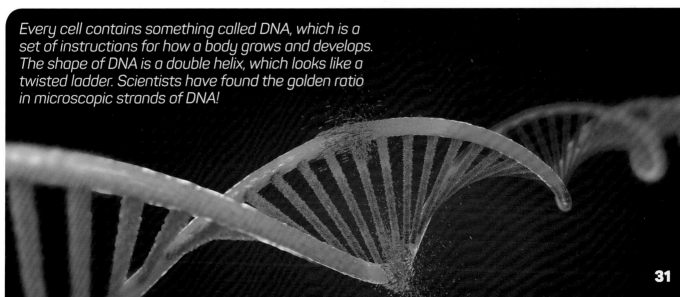

Every cell contains something called DNA, which is a set of instructions for how a body grows and develops. The shape of DNA is a double helix, which looks like a twisted ladder. Scientists have found the golden ratio in microscopic strands of DNA!

Index

The Author

Nancy Dickmann worked in publishing for many years before becoming a full-time author. Now, with Pushkin the Three-Legged Wonder Cat as her trusty assistant (in charge of lap-sitting), she writes books on a wide range of topics, including animals, space, history, health and explorers. The highlight of her career so far has been getting to interview a real astronaut to find out how they use the toilet in space!

Picture credits

(abbreviations: t = top; b = bottom; c = centre;
l = left; r = right)
Shutterstock: Alex Staroseltsev 11r, Anan Kaewkhammul 8l & 9r, Attila JANDI 2, Bachkova Natalia 1 & 23tl, Bildagentur Zoonar GmbH 24bl, BMJ 27cr, Brian Zanchi 12bl & 32r, ChameleonsEye 31tr, Christoph Burgstedt 31b, Dan Newman 17br, 21tr, 23br & 29cl, Danny Iacob 14, Djomas 9tl, Eugene Kalenkovich 10bl, feathercollector 26, Garmasheva Natalia 31, Harvepino 6bl, imtmphoto 31tl, Isabelle OHara 23cr &30l, isarescheewin 17cr, JONATHAN PLEDGER 25tl, Kichigin 20, Kostiantyn Kravchenko 16, Kuttelvaserova Stuchelova 8cr, Lee Torrens 19tl, Marcelle Robbins 26bl, naluwan 15br & 28tr, Picasa 15mr, RealNoi 7, Rich Carey 31cr, Rusla Ruseyn 3 & 12, S-F 18, Sergiy Kuzmin 17tr, Shebeko 4, steiluc 22, Steve Heap 27br & 29br, tolii_vec 9bl & 28cl, Tomatito 20bl, topseller 10, tr3gin 11br &28bl, Vladimir Melnik 24.